A ONE-YEAR STUDY OF THE HARMONY OF THE GOSPELS

Quarter 1

Arranged by Kevin L. Greer

Based upon J. W. McGarvey's *Harmony of the Gospels*

Lessons written by Kevin L. Greer and Kyle D. Frank

Gospel Armory
PUBLISHING

A One-Year Study of the Harmony of the Gospels: Quarter 1
Copyright © 2022

All Rights Reserved. No portion of this book may be reproduced in any form without the written permission of the publisher, except in the case of brief excerpts to be used in a review.

Published by:
Gospel Armory Publishing
Bowling Green, Kentucky
www.GospelArmory.com

Printed in the United States of America

ISBN: 978-1-942036-99-9

TABLE OF CONTENTS

INTRODUCTION		5
LESSON 1	INTRODUCTORY AND BACKGROUND MATERIAL John 1:1-18; Luke 1:1-4; Matthew 1:17; Luke 3:23-38	7
LESSON 2	FROM THE ANNUNCIATION OF THE BIRTH OF JOHN THE BAPTIST TO ZACHARIAH THROUGH JOSEPH'S DREAM CONCERNING MARY AND JESUS Luke 1:5-25, 26-38, 39-56, 57-80; Matthew 1:18-25	11
LESSON 3	FROM THE BIRTH OF JESUS THROUGH HIS PRESENTATION AT THE TEMPLE Luke 2:1-7, 8-20, 21-39	17
LESSON 4	THE INFANCY AND YOUTH OF JESUS Matthew 2:1-12, 13-18, 19-23; Luke 2:39, 40-52	21
LESSON 5	FROM THE BEGINNING OF THE MINISTRY OF JOHN THE BAPTIST THROUGH THE TEMPTATION OF CHRIST IN THE WILDERNESS Matthew 3:1-12; Mark 1:18; Luke 3:1-18 Matthew 3:13-17; Mark 1:9-11; Luke 3:21-23 Matthew 4:1-11; Mark 1:12-13; Luke 4:1-13	25
LESSON 6	FROM JOHN'S FIRST TESTIMONY ABOUT JESUS THROUGH JESUS' FIRST RESIDENCE AT CAPERNAUM John 1:19-34; 35-51; 2:1-11, 12	30
LESSON 7	FROM THE FIRST PASSOVER OF JESUS' MINISTRY THROUGH HIS LEAVING JUDEA FOR GALILEE John 2:13-25; 3:1-21, 22-36 Matthew 4:12; Mark 1:14; Luke 3:19-20; John 4:1-4	34

LESSON 8	FROM JESUS AT SYCHAR IN SAMARIA THROUGH HIS SECOND MIRACLE AT CANA John 4:4-52; Luke 4:14; John 4:43-45 Matthew 4:17; Mark 1:14-15; Luke 4:14-15; John 4:46-54	40
LESSON 9	FROM JESUS AT CAPERNAUM THROUGH THE HEALING OF PETER'S MOTHER-IN-LAW Matthew 4:13-16, 18-22; Mark 1:16-20; Luke 5:1-11 Mark 1:21-28; Luke 4:31-37 Matthew 8:14-17; Mark 1:29-34; Luke 4:38-41	45
LESSON 10	FROM JESUS' PREACHING TOUR THROUGH GALILEE THROUGH THE CALL OF MATTHEW (LEVI) Matthew 4:23-25; Mark 1:35-39; Luke 4:42-44 Matthew 8:2-4; Mark 1:40-45; Luke 5:12-16 Matthew 9:2-8; Mark 2:1-12; Luke 5:17-26 Matthew 9:9; Mark 2:13-14; Luke 5:27-28	48
LESSON 11	FROM THE SECOND PASSOVER OF JESUS' MINISTRY THROUGH HIS SELECTION OF THE TWELVE APOSTLES John 5:1-47; Matthew 12:1-8; Mark 2:23-28; Luke 6:1-5 Matthew 12:9-14; Mark 3:1-6; Luke 6:6-11 Matthew 12:15-21; Mark 3:7-12 Matthew 10:2-4; Mark 3:13-19; Luke 6:12-16	52
LESSON 12	THE SERMON ON THE MOUNT - PART ONE Matthew 5:1-16; Luke 6:17-26 Matthew 5:17-48; Luke 6:27-30, 32-36 Matthew 6:1-18	59
LESSON 13	THE SERMON ON THE MOUNT - PART TWO Matthew 6:19-34; 7:1-6; Luke 6:37-42; Matthew 7:7-11 Matthew 7:12; Luke 6:31; Matthew 7:13-23; Luke 6:43-45	64

INTRODUCTION

The gospels of Matthew, Mark, Luke, and John record the earthly life of Jesus. Throughout them we learn about His teachings and read about His miracles. They tell us of Jesus' death on the cross and His resurrection from the dead. These accounts were given so that we might understand that He was more than just a good man and a wise teacher. They were "written so that you may believe that Jesus is the Christ, the Son of God, and that by believing you may have life in his name" (John 20:31).

Taking J. W. McGarvey's work – *The Harmony of the Gospels* – this material progresses through the gospel accounts chronologically, arranging the four books in the order in which they occurred. As each gospel writer included different events, details, and points, studying all four together helps us to get a comprehensive picture of Jesus and His teaching. It has been divided into a one-year (fifty-two week) study, broken down into quarters of thirteen lessons each.

As you go through this study, be sure to read the passages that are given for each section in order to find the answers to the questions. Some questions are fairly straightforward while others require some critical thought or further study. The lessons are designed to help students – from children to adult, new converts to mature Christians – deepen their understanding of the gospels and strengthen their faith in Christ. The questions are based primarily on the English Standard Version, but there will be times when you will find it helpful to consult other translations (such as the King James Version).

LESSON 1
INTRODUCTORY AND BACKGROUND MATERIAL

Section A   **John's Introduction To The Gospel**
Read: John 1:1-18

1. Just as the Old Testament began with "In the beginning God…" (Genesis 1:1); the apostle John chose to start his part of the New Testament with the words: "In the _____ was the _____, and the Word was _____ _____, and the Word _____ God."

2. YES or NO (circle one) The Word is Jesus Christ; who is One with God the Father. {see also: Genesis 1:1; Exodus 3:13,14; John 8:58; John 10:30; and 1 John 5:7.}

3. In verses 3-5 of the passages; what are six things said about the Word (Christ)?

    i. _____

    ii. _____

    iii. _____

    iv. _____

    v. _____

    vi. _____

4. What was John the Baptist sent to do; and why? _____
_____

5. John was: (mark the correct answer)

    _____ that Light.

    _____ not sent from God.

    _____ sent to bear witness of that Light.

    _____ the one whose own received him not.

6. Who was preferred before John? _____;
   because _____

7. To as many as received Him Jesus gave the power to become sons of God; born: (mark the correct answer)

   _____ of blood.

   _____ of the will of the flesh.

   _____ of the will of man.

   _____ of God.

8. The Word was _____ _____ and dwelt among us, . . . and of _____ fulness have we received.

9. The law was given by Moses. What came by Jesus Christ? _____
   _____

10. (TRUE or FALSE) _____ At one time man has seen God.

Section B   Luke's Preface And Dedication
Read: Luke 1:1-4

1. YES or NO (circle one) When Luke wrote his account of the life and teachings of Christ, he was the first person to do so.

2. Give two reasons why Luke wrote:

   i. _____
   _____

   ii. _____
   _____

3. Those who had already "undertaken" to compile a narrative of the things that have been accomplished among us"…from the beginning were _____ and _____ of the word.

4. Using a good bible study reference work; find out what the name "Theophilus" means: _____; and what is known about him: _____

   _____

   _____

   _____

5. Theophilus is also mentioned: (mark the correct answer)

   _____ in another Gospel.

   _____ in the Epistles of Paul.

   _____ in the Book of Revelation.

   _____ in the Old Testament.

   _____ in the Book of Acts.

Section C   The Genealogies Of Jesus In Matthew And Luke
Read: Matthew 1:1-17; Luke 3:23-38

1. Matthew's genealogy starts with _____; but Luke's goes back farther, to show that Jesus is the _____ of _____.

2. Both genealogies prove that Jesus was descended from Abraham and from David the king; but which ancestor mentioned in both reveals that He was not of the official priestly line of Israel? _____

3. Besides Mary; what three other women are mentioned by name in the two accounts of the lineage of Jesus? Also, give scripture references as to where they are mentioned in the Old Testament:

   i. _____, found in _____

   ii. _____, found in _____

   iii. _____, found in _____

4. There is also another major difference in the two genealogies of Jesus. Using a good commentary or other reference work; explain this difference:

   _____

   _____

   _____

   _____

   _____

   _____

   _____

End of Lesson 1

LESSON 2
FROM THE ANNUNCIATION OF THE BIRTH OF JOHN THE BAPTIST TO ZACHARIAH THROUGH JOSEPH'S DREAM CONCERNING MARY AND JESUS

Section A The Annunciation Of The Birth Of John The Baptist
Read: Luke 1:5-25

1. (TRUE or FALSE) _____ Zachariah and his wife were both of the priestly lineage of the children of Israel.

2. Was the system of "divisions" of the priests originally set up at the establishment of the Levitical priesthood by Moses? _____ Look up the passage in the Old Testament where the courses of the priesthood were set up: _____
_____

3. Zachariah and Elizabeth were _____ _____ before God, _____ in all the commandments and statutes of the Lord.

4. Why did they not yet have any children? _____
_____

5. As Zachariah went into the temple, his lot was to: (mark the correct answer)

   _____ place the showbread on the table.

   _____ enter the Holy of Holies.

   _____ burn incense.

   _____ offer up a burnt offering.

6. The angel which appeared to Zechariah was named. _____
Where did he stand? _____

7. The angel's message was concerning Elizabeth bearing him a son. The son was to be called _____.

8. What were some of the things that were to be special about John?

_____

_____

_____

_____

9. (TRUE or FALSE) _____ John was really Elijah the prophet reborn.

10. What was the sign that was given to Zachariah that these things would come to pass? _____

_____

11. When Elizabeth conceived; she hid herself _____ months; and said the Lord had taken away her _____ _____ people.

Section B The Annunciation Of The Birth Of Jesus To Mary
Read: Luke 1:26-38

1. YES or NO (circle one) The same angel came to Mary that had appeared to Zachariah.

2. Mary was a _____ espoused (to be married) to a man named Joseph, of the house of _____.

3. The angel said, "_____ _____ _____ _____ the Lord is with you."

4. What did he say about what was going to happen to her? _____

_____

_____

_____

5. In explaining to Mary how she, a virgin, could conceive, the angel used her cousin _____ as an example of how with _____ nothing is impossible.

6. The angel was speaking in fulfillment of prophecy. Which passage of scripture contains that prophecy: (mark the correct answer)

   _____ Amos 9:11

   _____ Isaiah 7:14

   _____ Malachi 4:5, 6

   _____ Acts 21:10, 11

   _____ Deuteronomy 18:15

Section C **The Visit Of Mary To Elizabeth**
Read: Luke 1:39-56

1. In those days, Mary arose and went with haste, _____ _____ _____ _____ to a town in Judah; to the house of _____, and greeted _____.

2. (TRUE or FALSE) _____ When Elizabeth heard Mary's greeting her baby leaped in her womb; in keeping with the prophecy of the angel Gabriel in Luke 1:15.

3. Why was Elizabeth honored to be visited by Mary? _____
_____
_____

4. YES or NO (circle one) Elizabeth blessed Mary and told her that what the Lord had said would come to pass.

5. List as many things as you can that Mary said after "My soul magnifies the Lord, And my spirit rejoices in God my Savior…"

_____

_____

_____

_____

6. Mary stayed with Elizabeth about _____ months, then returned to her own home.

Section D   **The Birth And Early Life Of John The Baptist**
Read: Luke 1:57-80

1. John's birth was a time of great rejoicing for Zechariah, Elizabeth and all their neighbors and _____; and on the eighth day, when they came to circumcise the child; And the friends would have called him Zechariah, after the _____ of his _____, but his mother said "No; he shall be called _____."

2. Why did the friends and relatives take exception to the name John? _____
_____

3. Because of his doubting the angel's words concerning John's birth, he had been mute and unable to speak ; therefore Zechariah used what to answer the people as to what he would have the baby called: (mark the correct answer)

_____ a writing tablet.

_____ sign language.

_____ a letter left by the angel.

4. When Zachariah wrote "His name is John"; what seven things happened?

   i. _____

   ii. _____

   iii. _____

   iv. _____

   v. _____

   vi. _____

   vii. _____

5. (TRUE or FALSE) _____ Zachariah's song of praise and prophecy contained references to early promises of God, and to the future work and mission of his newborn son.

6. "And the child grew and _____ _____ in spirit, and he was in the _____ till the day of his _____ _____ to Israel."

Section E **Joseph's Dream Concerning Mary And Her Unborn Child**
Read: Matthew 1:18-25

1. Jesus' mother was espoused to Joseph, but was found to be with child (of the Holy Ghost). Such was considered the equivalent of adultery; and was punishable by death. But, Joseph was "a _____ man and _____ to put her to shame, resolved to _____ _____ quietly."

2. Was the angel which appeared to him in a dream named in the passage? _____

3. Why was Joseph told not to fear to take Mary unto him as his wife? _____
   _____
   _____

4. Yes or No (circle one) The birth of Jesus would be the fulfillment of prophecy.

5. Immanuel, being interpreted is: (mark the correct choice)

   _____ the sons of thunder.

   _____ God with us.

   _____ a stone.

   _____ the Lamb of God.

   _____ Saviour.

6. (Question for Class Discussion or for Private Meditation) What does the phrase "knew her not till she had brought forth her firstborn son..." indicate about the claim of the "perpetual virginity" of Mary?

End of Lesson 2

LESSON 3
FROM THE BIRTH OF JESUS THROUGH HIS PRESENTATION AT THE TEMPLE

Section A   **The Birth Of Jesus**
Read: Luke 2:1-7

1. Why did Joseph take his wife Mary, who was "great with child," from Nazareth to Bethlehem? _____

2. While they were in Bethlehem, and the time came for Jesus to be born; they had to take shelter in a manger, because: (mark the correct answer)

    _____ they were considered outcasts, because they came from Nazareth.

    _____ Joseph had spent all their money paying the tax.

    _____ God had told them not to stay at the inn.

    _____ there was no room for them in the inn.

3. "And she _____ _____ her firstborn son, and wrapped him in swaddling _____, and laid him in a _____."

Section B   **The Birth Of Jesus Is Proclaimed To The Shepherds**
Read: Luke 2:8-20

1. (TRUE or FALSE) _____ It was day when the angel of the Lord appeared.

2. Quote the message of the angel to the shepherds: _____

_____

_____

_____

_____

3. The heavenly host praised God, saying "_____ to God in the highest, and _____ on peace among those with whom he is pleased."

4. YES or NO (circle one) The shepherds went to Bethlehem to see the "thing which is come to pass;" but they were not able to find Joseph, Mary, and Jesus.

5. What did they do once they had seen Jesus; and what was the reaction of all that heard their story? _____

_____

_____

6. "But Mary treasured up _____ _____ _____, and pondering them in her heart."

Section C Jesus' Circumcision And Presentation At The Temple
Read: Luke 2:21-39

1. And at the end of eight days, when he was circumcised, he was called Jesus the name given by the angel before he was conceived in the womb. Verses 23 and 24 of the passage read state what requirements of the Law were to be met. Look up the passages in the Old Testament to which these verses refer:

_____

_____

_____

_____

2. Give three characteristics of Simeon:

    i. _____

    ii. _____

    iii. _____

3. It was revealed that he (Simeon) should _____ _____ death, before he had seen the Lord's Christ.

4. When he met the family in the temple, while he "came by the Spirit"; what did he say about:

    i. Himself? _____
    _____

    ii. God's salvation? _____
    _____

    iii. The child Jesus? _____
    _____

    ii. Mary? _____
    _____

5. Anna the prophetess, was a righteous widow of about 84 years who lived at the temple; fasting and praying. She also _____ _____ (Jesus) to all them that looked for _____ in Jerusalem.

6. After performing those things required by the Law; Joseph, Mary, and Jesus went to: (mark the correct choice)

   _____ Samaria.

   _____ their new home in Jerusalem.

   _____ Nazareth.

   _____ Jericho.

   _____ Bethlehem.

   _____ a place unrecorded in the Word of God.

7. "And the child grew and _____ _____, filled with _____. And the favor of God was upon him."

End of Lesson 3

LESSON 4
THE INFANCY AND YOUTH OF JESUS

Section A   The Visit Of The Wise Men (Magi)
Read: Matthew 2:1-12

1. The wise men came from the east to Jerusalem, "Saying, Where is he that is born _____ of the Jews? for we have _____ _____ _____ when it rose and have come to worship him."

2. (TRUE or FALSE) _____ When Herod the king heard this he was the only one concerned about it.

3. The chief priests and scribes were called together to tell Herod where Christ was to be born. They told him "In Bethlehem of Judea: for thus it is written by the prophet…" Which prophet were they referring to? (Give book, chapter, and verse to support your answer.) _____

4. Herod called the wise men privately, and asked them what time the star appeared. He then sent them to Bethlehem to search _____ for the young child; and when they had found him they were to "bring me _____ _____, that I too may come and worship him also."

5. Once they followed the star to where Jesus was; they fell down and worshipped Him; and presented Him gifts. Name the three gifts:

    i. _____

    ii. _____

    iii. _____

6. Why didn't these wise men return to King Herod? _____

Section B   The Flight Into Egypt And The Slaughter Of The Children In Bethlehem
Read: Matthew 2:13-18

1. How was Joseph warned to go into Egypt, and why? _____
   _____
   _____

2. This would serve to fulfill what Old Testament prophecy? (Give book, chapter, and verse)
   _____

3. Knowing what he did of Christ's birth from the chief priests and scribes, and of the time of the appearance of the star from the wise men; Herod, when they (the wise men) didn't return to tell him where Jesus was; ordered the death of all children in and around Bethlehem two years old and younger; intending to kill Him. (TRUE or FALSE) _____ The results of this tragedy are also found in prophecy.

4. Where is the passage in the Old Testament found, which deals with this?
   _____

Section C   The Return To Nazareth
Read: Matthew 2:19-23; Luke 2:39

1. Joseph learned of Herod's death in a _____.

2. Why did he take his family to Nazareth instead of into Judea? (mark the correct answer)

   _____ he was afraid, because he heard that Herod's son, Archelaus was reigning there

   _____ to fulfil prophecy

   _____ he was warned of God in a dream

   _____ all of the above

Section D   Jesus Living At Nazareth, And The Visit To Jerusalem At The Age Of Twelve
Read: Luke 2:40-52

1. "And the child grew, and _____ _____, _____ with wisdom; and the grace of _____ was upon him."

2. YES or No (circle one) Jesus' family did not attend the Passover feast at Jerusalem regularly.

3. When they attended the feast when Jesus was 12 years old, and had "fulfilled the days"; He stayed behind; but His parents did not know it until they had made _____ _____ _____ towards home; thinking he was with the group of relatives and acquaintances traveling with them.

4. Upon returning to Jerusalem to look for Jesus; they searched for Him for: (mark the correct answer)

   _____ two weeks.

   _____ five days.

   _____ three days.

   _____ eight days.

5. Where did they find him? _____

   What was He doing? _____
   _____

6. (TRUE or FALSE) _____ Jesus had made an impression on the doctors of the Law and all that heard him by his understanding and his answers.

7. When Mary scolded Him for the worry He had caused them; He said "How is it that you _____ me? _____ _____ not that I must be about Father's _____?"

8. Yes or No (circle one) After Jesus returned with them to Nazareth and "was subject to them" as He grew; Mary "kept all these sayings in her heart."

9. Name three things that Jesus "increased in" as He grew up:

   i. _____

   ii. _____

   iii. _____

End of Lesson 4

A ONE-YEAR STUDY OF THE HARMONY OF THE GOSPELS | QUARTER 1

LESSON 5
FROM THE BEGINNING OF THE MINISTRY OF JOHN THE BAPTIST THROUGH THE TEMPTATION OF CHRIST IN THE WILDERNESS

Section A   **John The Baptist — His Person And His Preaching**
Read: Matthew 3:1-12; Mark 1:1-8; Luke 3:1-18

1. John the Baptist was sent from _____, for a _____ of the Light, Who is _____ _____.

2. According to Luke's Gospel; at what time did the word of God come to John in the wilderness?

   _____

   _____

   _____

   _____

3. Where in the Old Testament are the prophecies mentioned in Mark 1:2, 3 found? (mark the correct answer)

   _____ Hosea 14:4, 5 and Isaiah 19:16, 17

   _____ Malachi 3:1 and Isaiah 40:3, 4

   _____ Amos 9:11-15 and Zechariah 13:1-4

   _____ 1 Chronicles 22:9, 10 and Jeremiah 23:36

   _____ none of the above

4. (TRUE or FALSE) _____ John wore fine clothing and ate only the best food.

5. YES or NO (circle one) John claimed that there was no greater prophet than himself.

6. He said, "I _____ _____ you with water… but he (speaking of Him Who should come after) "shall baptize you with the _____ _____ and with _____."

7. (TRUE or FALSE) _____ John preached repentance and the baptism of repentance for the remission of sins; "for the kingdom of heaven was at hand."

8. Were those who came to John only from Jerusalem? _____

9. John baptized those who confessed their sins primarily in: (mark the correct answer)

   _____ the Red Sea.

   _____ the pool of Siloam.

   _____ the Sea of Galilee.

   _____ the Dead Sea.

   _____ the River Jordan.

10. Why was John angered by the presence of so many Pharisees and Sadducees at his baptisms; and what did he say to them?

11. John said that He Who would come after Him would be mightier than he was and would do what six things?

   i. _____

   ii. _____

   iii. _____

   iv. _____

   v. _____

   vi. _____

12. What did John tell the following people when they asked him what to do:

   The people in general? _____
   _____

   The publicans? _____
   _____

   The soldiers? _____
   _____

13. YES or NO (circle one) The people all wondered if John were the Christ.

Section B **The Baptism Of Jesus By John**
Read: Matthew 3:13-17; Mark 1:9-11; Luke 3:21-23

1. Then Jesus came from _____ to _____ to John, to be baptized by him.

2. a. What was John's objection to baptizing Jesus? _____

_____

_____

b. What was Jesus' response? _____

_____

_____

3. Quote Matthew 3:16, 17:

_____

_____

_____

_____

_____

_____

_____

_____

Section C   **Jesus Is Tempted By Satan In The Wilderness**
Read: Matthew 4:1-11; Mark 1:12, 13; Luke 4:1-13

1. "Then Jesus was led up by the _____ into the wilderness to be tempted by the devil. And after he had _____ forty days and forty nights, he was _____."

2. Describe the three temptations of Jesus by Satan:

   i. _____

   _____

   ii. _____

   _____

   iii. _____

   _____

3. (TRUE or FALSE) _____ Jesus never once used scripture to counter the devil's attempts to cause him to sin; because, even though He was all man, He was also divine; therefore He didn't need to.

4. Did Satan ever tempt Christ again? (cite book, chapter, and verse)

   _____

   _____

End of Lesson 5

LESSON 6
FROM JOHN'S FIRST TESTIMONY ABOUT JESUS THROUGH JESUS' FIRST RESIDENCE AT CAPERNAUM

Section A John The Baptist's First Testimony About Jesus
Read: John 1:19-34

1. "...when the Jews sent priests and Levites from Jerusalem to ask him, 'Who are you?' He confessed, and _____ _____ _____ but confessed 'I am _____ _____ Christ.'"

2. What five questions did they then ask him about himself, that they might "give an answer to" those who sent them?

   i. _____

   ii. _____

   iii. _____

   iv. _____

   v. _____

3. What was his only reply; and what prophet did he quote? (cite book, chapter, and verse for the prophecy involved)

   _____
   _____
   _____

4. Yes or No (circle one) It was the Pharisees which were sent.

5. What were their next questions concerning? _____
   _____

6. (TRUE or FALSE) _____ In his answer, John pointed them to Christ.

7. "These things took place in _____ across _____ _____ where John was baptizing."

8. The next day John saw Jesus coming and said, "Behold the _____ of _____, who _____ _____ the sin of the world!"

9. John testified that Jesus was He of Whom he spoke; but, that he "I did not know him"; except by the fact the "he that sent me to baptize with water" had given him a sign; which was:

   _____
   _____
   _____
   _____

Section B **Jesus Makes His First Disciples**
Read: John 1:35-51

1. The next day after, John and two of his disciples were standing, and saw Jesus walking; and John said, "_____ _____ Lamb _____ _____!"

2. YES or NO (circle one) The two disciples followed Jesus and asked Him where he lived.

3. What was Jesus' answer? _____

4. One of the two disciples of John that followed Jesus that afternoon was _____, _____ _____ brother.

5. The next day Jesus found _____ as He went toward Galilee. Philip was from the same town as Andrew and Peter; which was _____.

6. Philip found Nathanael, and told him that _____
   _____

   "_____ of Nazareth, the son of Joseph."

7. YES or NO (circle one) Philip was highly impressed when he heard that Jesus was from Nazareth.

8. Philip told him to come and see for himself. When Jesus saw Nathanael coming, he said what?

   _____

   _____

9. When Nathanael asked Jesus how he knew him; Jesus said: _____

   _____

10. This convinced Nathanael that: (mark the correct answer)

    _____ Jesus was lying.

    _____ Jesus was nobody special.

    _____ Jesus was a publican.

    _____ Jesus was the Son of God, and King of Israel.

    _____ Jesus had an evil spirit of divination.

11. YES or NO (circle one) Because Nathanael believed on Jesus because He said that he saw him under the fig tree; Jesus told him he would see even greater things.

12. (Question for Class Discussion or for Personal Meditation) What does the first encounter between Jesus and Nathanael say about faith. (See: John 20:29 and Hebrews 11:1-40; see also 1 Corinthians 13:13 and James 2:19-26)

Section C **Jesus Works His First Miracle At Cana In Galilee**
Read: John 2:1-11

1. The next day (the third day) there was a marriage in Cana of Galilee. Jesus' mother was there. Jesus was also invited, and His disciples, also. There was a problem at the marriage feast, and Mary wanted Jesus to help. What was His response, and what did He do regarding the lack of wine?

   _____

   _____

   _____

   _____

   _____

2. The first miracle was a success in the physical sense; but, more importantly, it was a success for Him in His ministry, because he "manifested _____ glory; and his _____ believed on him."

Section D **Jesus' First Residence At Capernaum**
Read: John 2:12

1. "After this he went down to _____, and his _____, and his brethren, and his _____; and they stayed there _____ _____ _____ days."

2. Because of the number of times He stayed there during His ministry, it is thought that Capernaum, more or less, became Jesus' primary residence, or "home base" during much of his teaching and preaching while on earth. Using a few good Bible Study reference works, such as a Bible map book or atlas, or a Bible encyclopedia; find out what you can about Capernaum in Jesus' day, and what became of it in later history.

End of Lesson 6

LESSON 7
FROM THE FIRST PASSOVER OF JESUS' MINISTRY THROUGH HIS LEAVING JUDEA FOR GALILEE

Section A Jesus' First Cleansing Of The Temple
Read: John 2:13-25

1. "The passover of the Jews was at hand, and Jesus went up to _____."

2. What did He find in the temple?

   i. _____

   ii. _____

3. How did He drive the livestock out of the temple? (mark the correct answer)

   _____ with a shepherd's staff

   _____ with a sword

   _____ with a spear

   _____ with a scourge (small whip) that He had made

4. YES or NO (circle one) Jesus did nothing about the moneychangers.

5. (TRUE or FALSE) _____ At this time, Jesus said the Jews had made the temple a "den of thieves."

6. Where is it written "The zeal for your house will consume me"? (cite book, chapter, and verse)

   _____

7. Seeing Jesus do these things, the Jews demanded a sign of the authority by which he did them. Jesus answered them, "_____ this temple, and in three _____ I will _____ _____ up."

8. The temple at Jerusalem had thus far taken forty-six years to build (and was still being completed), and the Jews, not knowing that Jesus was _____ of the "temple of _____ _____ said;" "you will _____ _____ _____ in three days?"

9. When did his disciples remember this incident, and what did it cause them to do?

_____

_____

_____

10. (TRUE or FALSE) _____ Even though many believed on Jesus, when they saw the miracles He did at the passover; He did not commit himself to them because He feared the Sanhedrin.

Section B **Jesus Talks With Nicodemus**
Read: John 3:1-21

1. Nicodemus, a Pharisee and a ruler of the Jews, came to Jesus by night (privately). What reason did he give for admitting that the Jews knew that Jesus was "a teacher come from God"?

_____

_____

2. Quote Jesus' response:

_____

_____

_____

_____

3. Nicodemus could not understand how a man could be born again. He said, How can a man _____ the _____ _____ into his mother's _____ and be born?

4. Jesus told him that the only way for a man to enter then kingdom of God was to be born of: (mark the correct answer)

    _____ the Father and the Son.

    _____ the body and blood of Christ.

    _____ the blood and water.

    _____ the water and the Spirit.

    _____ none of the above.

5. What example did Christ use to show Nicodemus why he should not marvel at His saying "You must be born again?"

    _____

    _____

    _____

6. (TRUE or FALSE) _____ When Nicodemus still did not understand, Jesus said that it because of his spiritual blindness and prejudices as a master of Israel.

7. YES or NO (circle one) Christ told Nicodemus that He spoke what He knew, and that if he told him of earthly things and would not believe, how could he believe if he was told of heavenly things.

8. Jesus then told Nicodemus three other things about Himself. What were they?

   i. _____

   ii. _____

   iii. _____

9. (Question for Class Discussion or Private Meditation) Much has been made of the love of God for the world (John 3:16-21) and how simple and easy it is to just believe on Jesus Christ and be saved. Is there more to saving faith than just giving the mental assent to the fact (having the belief) that Jesus Christ is the Son of God Who gave Himself on the cross to save the sinners of the world?

Section C   Jesus' First Ministry In Judea And John's Second Testimony
Read: John 3:22-36

1. Verse 22 says that Jesus and his disciples came into Judea and stayed for a time, "and baptized." Did Jesus himself baptize anyone personally? Look up (and cite book, chapter, and verse for) any passages pertinent to the question.

   _____

   _____

   _____

   _____

2. YES or NO (circle one) Was John, at this time, in prison?

3. In the question between John's disciples and the Jews about purifying; the Jews said that Christ was baptizing; and that "all men come to him"; perhaps to stir up jealousy between John and his disciples; and Jesus and His. John made seven comments in reply:

   i. _____

   ii. _____

   iii. _____

   iv. _____

   v. _____

   vi. _____

   vii. _____

4. (TRUE or FALSE) _____ He that is from the earth is earthly; but He that cometh from heaven is above all.

5. YES or NO (circle one) John said all man received His (Christ's) testimony.

6. He that has received his testimony to his seal that is true.

7. YES or NO (circle one) Christ's words came from God and God gave Him the Spirit without measure.

8. (TRUE or FALSE) _____ God did not give all things to Jesus.

9. To believe on Christ is to have everlasting life. What is said about unbelief?

   _____

   _____

   _____

Section D **Jesus Sets Out From Judea For Galilee**
Read: Matthew 4:12; Mark 1:14; Luke 3:19, 20; John 4:1-4

1. YES or NO (circle one) When Jesus found out that the Jews knew He (his disciples) were baptizing more disciples than John; he left Judea, and went back to Galilee.

2. He also left because _____ was cast into prison.

3. Who had put John in prison? _____

4. To get to Galilee, Christ went through _____.

End of Lesson 7

LESSON 8
FROM JESUS AT SYCHAR IN SAMARIA THROUGH HIS SECOND MIRACLE AT CANA

Section A At Jacob's Well At Sychar
Read: John 4:4-52

1. At Sychar, in Samaria, Jesus was sitting on Jacob's well when a Samaritan woman came to draw water. When Jesus asked her to give Him some water to drink, she was surprised that a Jew would ask a Samaritan for a drink; because "for Jews _____ _____ _____ with _____."

2. Quote Jesus' reply:

   _____
   _____
   _____
   _____

3. (TRUE or FALSE) _____ The woman knew what Jesus meant by "living water."

4. In response to her questions, Jesus told her what three things?

   i. _____
   _____

   ii. _____
   _____

   iii. _____
   _____

A ONE-YEAR STUDY OF THE HARMONY OF THE GOSPELS | QUARTER 1

5. When the woman asked for the "living water"; Jesus said to her: (mark the correct answer)

   _____ "It is not right to take the children's bread, and throw it to the dogs."

   _____ "Daughter, your faith has made you well."

   _____ "Go, call your husband, and come here."

   _____ none of the above.

6. YES or NO (circle one) When the Samaritan woman admitted that she had no husband; and Jesus told her that she had spoken the truth; because she had had five husbands; and the man that she had was not her husband; the Samaritan woman asked Jesus how He knew all this.

7. When she talked of how the Samaritans "worshipped on this mountain"; but that the Jews said Jerusalem was the place "where people ought to worship"; Jesus told her that when the kingdom would come ("the hour comes"); men would worship neither in "this mountain, nor at Jerusalem;" but that "what we _____; for salvation is of _____ _____."

8. (TRUE or FALSE) _____ Jesus then told her how true worshippers should worship God.

9. Describe "true worship" and why God seeks it.

_____

_____

_____

_____

_____

_____

_____

10. When the woman heard these things, she acknowledged that she expected the Messiah would come and "_____ _____ _____ things."

11. When Christ revealed to her that He was the Messiah, the woman: (mark the correct answer)

    _____ bowed down and worshipped Him.

    _____ went away into the city and told the men what had happened, and asked them "Is this not the Christ?"

    _____ said, "Depart from me, for I am a sinner!"

    _____ ran away in fear.

12. YES or NO (circle one) Many of the Samaritans did not believe on Jesus for what the woman had said; and asked him to depart out of their country.

13. After reading verses 32 through 38, quote verse 34; and explain what Jesus meant by "I have food to eat that you do not know about":

    _____
    _____
    _____
    _____
    _____
    _____

14. (TRUE or FALSE) _____ After staying there for two days; more Samaritans believed; but only because of the woman's testimony.

Section B   **Jesus' Arrival In Galilee**
                 Read: Luke 4:14; John 4:43-45

1. YES or NO (circle one) Jesus returned in the power of the Spirit into Galilee.

2. When He came into Galilee, Jesus knew that "a _____ has no _____ _____ his own _____."

3. Yet, his fame spread throughout the region, by virtue of the _____ having seen all the _____ that he _____ at _____ at the feast.

Section C   **Jesus' Teaching In Galilee**
                 Read: Matthew 4:17; Mark 1:14, 15; Luke 4:14, 15

1. "From that time Jesus _____ to _____, and to say _____, _____: the _____ _____ _____ is at hand."

2. YES or NO (circle one) John the Baptist was free from prison at this time.

3. What else did Jesus call on people to do? _____

4. (TRUE or FALSE) _____ Jesus did not teach in any of the synagogues in Galilee.

Section D   **The Second Miracle At Cana**
                 Read: John 4:46-54

1. Yes or No (circle one) The nobleman's son was sick at Nazareth.

2. When the nobleman sought Jesus that he might heal his son, who was at the point of death; Jesus told him that, "except you see" what two things, "you will not believe"?

       i. _____

       ii. _____

3. Jesus said, "Go, your son will live." "The man _____ the _____ Jesus had _____ to him." On his way home, his servants met him and told him that his son's fever left him at the same hour Jesus had said.

End of Lesson 8

A ONE-YEAR STUDY OF THE HARMONY OF THE GOSPELS | QUARTER 1

LESSON 9
FROM JESUS AT CAPERNAUM THROUGH THE HEALING OF PETER'S MOTHER-IN-LAW

Section A   **Jesus At Capernaum**
   Read: Matthew 4:13-16

1. Capernaum was on the coast of what sea? _____

2. It was also within the borders of _____ and _____, which fulfilled a prophecy of Isaiah. Look up this prophecy and give the chapter and verses in which it is found:

   _____

   _____

3. Quote Verse 16:

   _____

   _____

   _____

4. YES or NO (circle one) This is the point at which Christ began to preach repentance and the coming of the kingdom of heaven.

Section B   **The Call Of Four Fishermen**
   Read: Matthew 4:18-22; Mark 1:16-20; Luke 5:1-11

1. Walking along the coast of the sea of Galilee; Jesus saw two of his disciples, the brothers Simon (called Peter) and Andrew casting a fishing net into the sea. He said, "_____ _____, and I will make you _____ _____ men." And they left _____ _____, and followed Him.

2. He then saw two other brothers, the sons of Zebedee, in a ship with their father, mending their nets; and called them, too. They names were _____ and _____; and they left their father in the ship with the _____ _____, and also followed Jesus.

3. (TRUE or FALSE) _____ Luke's version of the call of Peter, Andrew, James and John includes a miraculous event.

4. In Luke's account, the miracle caused Peter to fall down at Jesus' knees and say "Depart from me; for I am a _____ _____, O Lord."

Section C **Jesus Casts Out A Demon In A Synagogue**
Read: Mark 1:21-28; Luke 4:31-37

1. YES or NO (circle one) When Jesus taught on the sabbath days in the synagogue at Capernaum, few people were impressed with His doctrine.

2. A man with an unclean (spirit, or demon) was at the synagogue one day. What four things did the demon say to Jesus?

    i. _____

    ii. _____

    iii. _____

    iv. _____

3. Jesus rebuked the unclean spirit, saying "_____ _____ of him." The demon threw the man down in the midst of the people, "came out of him, and _____ Him not."

4. YES or NO (circle one) Jesus told the spirit not to speak.

5. What was the reaction of those who witnessed this: (mark the correct answer)

    _____ they were all amazed at Jesus' power and authority over unclean spirits

    _____ they rebuked Jesus for healing on the sabbath day

    _____ they demanded even greater miracles

    _____ all of the above

6. (TRUE or FALSE) _____ This incident gave Jesus a bad reputation among all the people in the country round about.

Section D The Healing Of Peter's Mother-In-Law And Many Others
Read: Matthew 8:14-17; Mark 1:29-34; Luke 4:38-41

1. When they left the synagogue, Jesus went with Peter, Andrew, James and John into Peter's house; but Peter's mother-in-law was sick with a _____.

2. (TRUE or FALSE) _____ When they asked Jesus to help her He rebuked the fever, and she was able to sleep peacefully.

3. At the end of the day many that were sick were brought to Jesus, and he healed them by: (mark the correct answer)

    _____ prayer and fasting.

    _____ saying, "Talitha cumi."

    _____ anointing their eyes with clay.

    _____ none of the above.

4. YES or NO (circle one) When he cast out demons, he let them tell everyone Who He was.

End of Lesson 9

LESSON 10
FROM JESUS' PREACHING TOUR THROUGH GALILEE THROUGH THE CALL OF MATTHEW (LEVI)

Section A **Jesus Makes A Preaching Tour Through Galilee**
Read: Matthew 4:23-25; Mark 1:35-39; Luke 4:42-44

1. Very early the next morning Jesus went out and _____ into a _____ place and _____.

2. When Simon and the rest found Him and told Him "All men seek you;" Jesus told them He wanted to go into the next towns, to _____ there _____. Why?

3. The people where he was wanted Him to stay with them but Jesus said what two about this?

    i. _____

    ii. _____

4. YES or NO (circle one) Jesus healed so many and cast out so many demons that great multitudes began to follow Him from many parts of the region; but they would not let Him preach in their synagogues.

Section B **Jesus Heals A Leper**
Read: Matthew 8:2-4; Mark 1:40-45; Luke 5:12-16

1. A leper came to Jesus and said "Lord, if _____ will, you can _____ _____."

2. (TRUE or FALSE) _____ Jesus did not touch the leper, but merely spoke the word, and he was healed.

3. Jesus then sent him to show himself to the priest and make an offering for his cleansing. Look up in the Old Testament (cite book, chapter, and verse) what this offering consisted of:

   _____

   _____

   _____

4. Although Jesus charged him to tell no man; the healed leper _____ _____, and began to _____ _____ much, and to blaze about the matter, so much so that Jesus could _____ _____ _____ into the city; and, even though He was out in the desert places, _____ came to Him from every _____.

5. Despite this fact; his fame caused one extra positive thing, which was that people came to _____ Him.

Section C **Jesus Heals A Paralyzed Man At Capernaum**
Read: Matthew 9:2-8; Mark 2:1-12; Luke 5:17-26

1. On a certain day; as Jesus was teaching; Pharisees and doctors of the law were sitting by; having come out of _____ town of _____, and _____, and Jerusalem; and Jesus was healing people with the _____ of the Lord.

2. There was brought to where Jesus was a man taken with a palsy (paralysis) to be healed; but those that carried him on his bed could not get in for the crowd. Relate the story of how they got the man to Jesus to be healed:

   _____

   _____

   _____

   _____

3. Instead of healing the man immediately, Jesus said "Take heart my son, your _____ _____ _____."

4. When the scribes and Pharisees said within themselves "This man blasphemes;" what did they mean?

   _____

   _____

5. Jesus, knowing their thoughts, said what?

   _____

   _____

   _____

6. (TRUE or FALSE) _____ To prove His point, Jesus used scripture to refute the Pharisees.

7. When Jesus healed the man; the multitudes saw it, and they did what three things?

   i. _____

   ii. _____

   iii. _____

Section D   The Call Of Matthew (Levi)
Read: Matthew 9:9; Mark 2:13, 14; Luke 5:27, 28

1. After He had healed the palsied man; Jesus came upon Matthew, sitting at _____ _____ of _____; and called him to follow Him.

2. YES or NO (circle one) Matthew, also called Levi, was a publican; a tax collector for the Romans.

3. Mark mentions that Matthew was also called _____, the son of _____.

4. Luke says that, when Jesus called him, Matthew "_____ _____ a _____ Him."

End of Lesson 10

LESSON 11
FROM THE SECOND PASSOVER OF JESUS' MINISTRY THROUGH HIS SELECTION OF THE TWELVE APOSTLES

Section A Jesus Heals On The Sabbath Day
Read: John 5:1-47

1. There was a feast of the Jews; and Jesus went up to Jerusalem; where there was, by the sheep market a pool called in Hebrew, Bethesda. There were at the place a great multitude of sick and infirm people who were:

    i. _____

    ii. _____

    iii. _____

2. They waited for the troubling of the waters. Why?

    _____
    _____
    _____

3. The man Jesus saw had had an infirmity for how many years? (mark the correct answer)

    _____ above 40 years

    _____ 12 years

    _____ 38 years

    _____ 18 years

    _____ none of the above

4. (TRUE or FALSE) _____ He had been prevented from entering the pool at the certain times the angel troubled the water; because he had always been asleep when it happened.

5. When Jesus learned of how long he had the infirmity; He asked him, "_____ _____ be made whole?"

6. The man answered and told him the reason he was unable to get into the pool to be healed, but Jesus said, "Rise, _____ _____ your bed, and _____. He was healed and he took up his bed and walked. This was on the sabbath day.

7. When the Jews saw the cured man, they accused him of breaking the Sabbath by carrying his bed. When he told them that he was doing what Jesus had commanded him; they asked him Who told him to "Take up your _____, and _____." He did not know Who had healed him, and, as Jesus was among a great multitude, had left the area.

8. YES or NO (circle one) When Jesus later found the man that He had cured, in the temple, He told him not to tell the Jews Who it was that had healed him, "Lest a worse thing come unto thee."

9. When the man told the Jews learned that it was Jesus Who had healed him on the Sabbath day; they began to:

   i. _____

   ii. _____

10. In addition, quote the verse in which Jesus said something that made the Jews all the more determined to kill Him:

    _____

    _____

11. YES or NO (circle one) Jesus claimed He did these things of His own power; and that even greater works would follow.

12. "For as the _____ raises the dead, and _____ _____ _____; even also the Son _____ _____ to _____ _____ _____."

13. (TRUE or FALSE) _____ The Father judges man, but has not committed any judgement to the Son; and the Father should be honored, but not the Son; and to dishonor the Son in no way dishonors the Father which sent Him.

14. In verses 24 through 26: relate the sayings that start off with the words, "Truly, Truly":

___

___

___

___

___

15. Jesus told the people to "Do not marvel" at these things, because the hour was coming that all those in the graves would hear His voice; and come forth to one of two different resurrections:

    Those that have done good, to the resurrection of _____.

    Those that have done evil, to the resurrection of _____.

16. (TRUE or FALSE) _____ Jesus admitted that He could do nothing of His own self, nor did He bear witness of Himself.

17. Who were two that bore witness of Christ? _____ and Jesus' _____.

18. YES or NO (circle one) John was the greater witness.

19. The _____ _____, which sent Him, also bore witness to Christ.

20. Quote Verse 39:

___

___

___

21. (TRUE or FALSE) _____ The Jews believed in Christ because He came in His Father's name; but did not believe others whom came in their own name.

22. Jesus told the Jews that He did not _____ _____ to the Father; but that _____, in whom they trusted, accused them.

23. If they had _____ Moses; they would have believed _____, for Moses of Him. But, if they would not believe Moses' _____, how could they believe His _____?

Section B   **The Defense Of The Disciples Who Plucked Grain On The Sabbath**
Read: Matthew 12:1-8; Mark 2:23-28; Luke 6:1-5

1. Relate the incident which prompted the Pharisees to accuse Jesus' disciples of doing that which was unlawful.

   _____

   _____

   _____

2. This act of the disciples was a violation of: (mark the correct answer)

   _____ the Ten Commandments.

   _____ the traditions of the Jewish Fathers.

   _____ the Law of Moses.

   _____ the decrees of Caesar.

3. What Old Testament passage makes up the basis of Christ's defense of His disciples? (cite book, chapter, and verse)

   _____

   _____

4. In Matthew's account, Jesus also mentioned how the _____ in the _____ _____ the and were blameless. Look up this reference as well.

5. (TRUE or FALSE) _____ Matthew, Mark and Luke all state that Jesus said that the Son of Man is Lord of the Sabbath, and Mark adds that the Sabbath was made for man, and not man for the Sabbath.

6. Matthew's account also contains two other additional statements? They are:

   i. _____

   ii. _____

Section C **Jesus Heals A Man With A Withered Hand**
Read: Matthew 12:9-14; Mark 3:1-6; Luke 6:6-11

1. When Jesus was in the synagogue, there was a man with withered hand; those who sought that "they might _____ Him" tempting Him by asking Jesus, "Is it _____ to _____ on the _____ _____?"

2. From Verse 11 and 12 of Matthew; quote Jesus' response:

   _____
   _____
   _____
   _____
   _____

3. Mark and Luke relate that Jesus asked, "Is it _____ to do good on the sabbath days, or _____ _____? to save life, or to kill (destroy it)?"

4. (TRUE or FALSE) _____ When they refused to answer Him; Jesus was angry; "grieved at the hardness of heart"; and then He healed the man.

5. From that time onward, being _____ with _____, the _____ and the _____ took counsel (communed together) how that they might _____ Him.

Section D   **Jesus Heals The Multitudes Beside The Sea Of Galilee**
Read: Matthew 12:15-21; Mark 3:7-12

1. In His healing of the multitudes which followed Him, Jesus charged them that they should not make it known. This was in the fulfillment of the prophecy of Isaiah in what chapter and verses?

   _____

2. (Question for Class Discussion or Personal Meditation) Why else would Jesus not want His healing known at this time? (See: John 2:4; and also, John 2:23-25)

Section E   **Jesus Selects Twelve Apostles**
Read: Matthew 10:2-4; Mark 3:13-19; Luke 6:12-16

1. Jesus' apostles were twelve men from among his disciples; to whom he gave what two powers?

   i. _____

   ii. _____

2. Before choosing the twelve; Jesus _____ _____ into a mountain to _____, and _____ all night in _____ to _____.

3. The names of the twelve are listed differently by Matthew, Mark, and Luke. List them here:

	Matthew	Mark	Luke
1.	_____	_____	_____
2.	_____	_____	_____
3.	_____	_____	_____
4.	_____	_____	_____
5.	_____	_____	_____
6.	_____	_____	_____
7.	_____	_____	_____
8.	_____	_____	_____
9.	_____	_____	_____
10.	_____	_____	_____
11.	_____	_____	_____
12.	_____	_____	_____

4. How many sets of brothers were there among the Apostles? (mark the correct answer)

   _____ four

   _____ one

   _____ three

   _____ two

   _____ there were none

5. (TRUE or FALSE) _____ Jesus gave them special powers, but forbade them to preach.

6. YES or NO (circle one) Judas Iscariot is named a traitor in only two of the accounts.

End of Lesson 11

A ONE-YEAR STUDY OF THE HARMONY OF THE GOSPELS | QUARTER 1

LESSON 12
THE SERMON ON THE MOUNT — PART ONE

Section A   **Introductory Statements, The Beatitudes, Blessings And Woes, The Salt Of The Earth, And The Light Of The World**
Read: Matthew 5:1-16; Luke 6:17-26

1. "And seeing the _____, he went _____ _____ _____ _____: and when he sat down, his _____ came unto him: And he opened his mouth, and taught them…"

2. The Beatitudes (or "declarations of blessedness") start with the saying "Blessed are" nine times; and once with the statement "Rejoice, and be glad." State these ten "declarations" and the reasons Jesus gives for each one.

   i. _____

   ii. _____

   iii. _____

   iv. _____

   v. _____

   vi. _____

   vii. _____

   viii. _____

   ix. _____

   x. _____

3. In Luke, in the "sermon in the plain," which is many ways similar to the sermon on the mount; Jesus had stood with "his disciples, and a great _____ of people out of _____ _____ and Jerusalem, and from the seacoast of _____ and _____, which came to _____ _____;" and to be healed of diseases and _____ _____.

4. In that account, Jesus told the multitudes they would be "blessed" under _____ (how many?) circumstances; and to "Rejoice" and "_____ _____ _____," for what reason?

_____

_____

5. (TRUE or FALSE) _____ In Luke's account, Jesus also pronounced four woes upon various ones, who are sad, hungry, poor, and persecuted in this life.

6. YES or NO (circle one) If those who follow Christ are the salt of the earth; they can never lose their savor.

7. Christians are also called the _____ of the _____; a city which is set on a _____ that cannot be _____.

8. We are to let our light so shine before men, that they may: (mark the two correct answers)

_____ see our spiritual and moral superiority.

_____ see our good works.

_____ view the church reproachfully.

_____ seek to be like us in serving God.

_____ glorify our heavenly Father.

Section B   **The Relation Of Jesus' Teaching To That Of The Old Testament Law And Jewish Traditions**
Read: Matthew 5:17-48; Luke 6:27-30, 32-36

1. (TRUE or FALSE) _____ Jesus came to destroy the law of Moses with His teaching.

2. Quote Matthew 5:18, 19.

___

3. YES or NO (circle one) Jesus taught that the righteousness of the scribes and Pharisees was unimportant.

4. (TRUE or FALSE) _____ Anger with a brother without cause is a serious matter.

5. (Question for Group Discussion or for Private Meditation) Why is just loving your friends and doing good to those who do the same to you not good enough in the kingdom of the Lord?

6. YES or NO (circle one) Adultery can only be committed in the act itself.

7. What two body parts were mentioned as better to cut off and lose than to lose one's soul in hell?

   _____ the ear and the nose

   _____ the hair and the arm

   _____ the eye and the right hand

   _____ the big toe and the index finger

8. Why is it best to let one's communication be "Yes" or "no"?

___

9. Cite at least two other passages of scripture that teach the same lesson concerning divorce as Matthew 5:31, 32.

_____

_____

10. Yes or No (circle one) "An eye for an eye, and a tooth for a tooth" has been replaced as the proper manner of settling personal wrongs.

Section C   **The Proper Manner Of Giving Alms, Prayer, And Fasting**
Read: Matthew 6:1-18

1. (TRUE or FALSE) _____ Giving or doing alms publicly has no rewards whatsoever.

2. Why should alms (charity) be done privately? (mark the correct answer)

    _____ because the Father which sees in secret will reward you openly

    _____ because to do so openly is blasphemy against the Holy Spirit

    _____ because even the heathen and sinners do that openly

    _____ because giving is only to be done while assembled with the saints upon the first day of the week

3. YES or NO (circle one) Ostentatious, "showy" prayer is allowable for the Christian because the world needs to see how righteous we are.

4. "_____ Father _____ what you have need of, _____ you ask Him."

5. Quote Matthew 6:17-18

_____

_____

_____

6. YES or NO (circle one) The last passage no longer applies because we are no longer under the law of Moses.

End of Lesson 12

LESSON 13
THE SERMON ON THE MOUNT — PART TWO

Section A **Earthly Worries Contrasted With The Security Of Heavenly Treasure**
Read: Matthew 6:19-34

1. If we lay up treasures on earth for ourselves; what three things does Jesus teach that can cause us concern?

    i. _____

    ii. _____

    iii. _____

2. YES or NO (circle one) Jesus teaches us in this passage not to be concerned with any kind of treasure.

3. "_____ where your _____ is, there will _____ heart _____ also."

4. If our eye is single our whole body is full of light; but if our eye is evil our body will be full of: (mark the correct answer)

    _____ much contentment.

    _____ great darkness.

    _____ abounding joy.

    _____ shameful sadness.

5. (TRUE or FALSE) _____ Verse 24 is summed up by the saying: "You cannot serve God and money."

6. In teaching about worldly cares, Jesus uses the examples of the _____ of the air and the _____ of _____ _____.

7. YES or NO (circle one) God doesn't take into account our daily, earthly needs.

8. Quote verse 33:

   _____

   _____

   _____

9. (TRUE or FALSE) _____ Verse 34 prohibits any kind of planning for the future. (See: Luke 14:27-33; 2 Corinthians 9:7; and 1 Timothy 5:8)

Section B **Concerning Judging Of Others**
Read: Matthew 7:1-6; Luke 6:37-42

1. To judge someone guilty of a sin when you yourself are guilty of a greater sin is to commit: (mark the correct answer)

   _____ idolatry.

   _____ blasphemy.

   _____ hypocrisy.

   _____ gossip.

2. Yes or No (circle one) Judging with righteous judgment is never allowable to the child of God.

3. We are judged as (or with the same type of judgment) we judge. Matthew states: with _____ _____ you give, it shall be _____ _____ you again"; while Luke states this concept as Judge not, and _____ _____ not _____ _____: _____ not, and you shall not be condemned: forgive _____ _____, and be _____.

4. (TRUE or FALSE) _____ Luke 6:38 refers to proper judgment and forgiveness.

5. Quote the parable in Luke 6:39, 40 that Matthew does not include:

   _____
   _____
   _____
   _____
   _____
   _____

6. YES or NO (Circle one) Matthew 7:6 has no bearing on judging others whatsoever.

Section C   **Concerning Prayer**
Read: Matthew 7:7-11

1. If we ask, it will be _____

   If we seek, we will _____

   If we knock, it will be _____

2. YES or NO (circle one) These things relating to our prayer are so important to understand that they are restated in verse 8.

3. What two items are mentioned as not being given to a son who asks for food?

   i. _____

   ii. _____

4. Why should we expect God to give us good things (according to this passage)?

   _____
   _____
   _____
   _____

Section D   **The Golden Rule**
Read: Matthew 7:12; Luke 6:31

1. (Question for Class Discussion or Personal Meditation) Other religions and philosophical systems have great rules similar to the Christian's "Golden Rule." They are generally expressed as: "Do not do unto others as you would not have others do unto you." Notice the difference. In what ways is Christ's teaching superior to that of others regarding this line of thought?

Section E   **Concerning The Two Ways And Discerning False Teachers**
Read: Matthew 7:13-23; Luke 6:43-45

1. (TRUE or FALSE) _____ "Easy" religion and "cheap" grace are in great demand; therefore there will never be more who will enter in the wide gate and travel the broad way; than those who will find the way which leads to life eternal.

2. YES or NO (circle one) False prophets will not always be known by their fruits and recognized as such; and some souls will unfortunately be lost to them.

3. Quote Luke 6:45:

_____

_____

_____

_____

_____

Section F   **Conclusion And Application — The Two Builders**
Read: Matthew 7:24-29; Luke 6:46-49

1. (TRUE or FALSE) _____ Jesus concludes His sermon by using the examples of the wise and foolish builders to show that just hearing the word is not enough, that action must be taken upon it, and application made of it.

2. The wise builder (the one who both hears and applies (obeys) Jesus' words) dug deep and _____ _____ _____ on a _____; and his house _____ against the flood.

3. The foundation (or rock) to build on wisely is the _____ of _____; lesser foundations fail, and lead to _____ _____.

4. "And when Jesus finished these _____ the crowds were astonished _____ _____. For he was teaching _____ as one _____ _____ _____ and not as the scribes."

End of Lesson 13

Made in the USA
Coppell, TX
10 December 2024